JESUS IS BORN

LeeDell Stickler

Illustrated by Suzanne Snider

Abingdon Press

Nashville

Jesus Is Born

ISBN 0-687-09560-3

This story is based on Matthew 1:18–2:12; Luke 1:26-38, 2:1-38

97 98 99 00 01 02 03 04 05 06 — 10 9 8 7 6 5 4 3 2 1

MANUFACTURED IN HONG KONG

This book is dedicated to the memory of Suzanne Snider,
whose art has touched the lives
of children around the world.

*L*ong ago in Bible times the people waited for a Savior. God had promised to send someone, a Messiah, who would save the people. The people trusted God's promise and looked forward to that time. As they waited, sometimes they wondered who would be the parents of that special child.

In the village of Nazareth there lived a young girl whose name was Mary. Mary was engaged to marry Joseph, the carpenter of the village. For now, Mary lived with her mother and her father. But one day soon, Mary would go to Joseph's house to live.

One day as Mary did her chores, a bright light filled the room. Suddenly an angel was standing before her.

"Greetings, Mary," said the angel. "The Lord is with you."

Now, Mary was afraid. She had never talked to an angel before.

"Do not be afraid," said the angel. "God has chosen you to be the mother of God's only son. You will name him Jesus."

"How can this be?" Mary asked. "I am not yet married to Joseph."

"Your child will be from God," said the angel. "With God, nothing is impossible."

"I am God's servant. Let it be just as you say," said Mary.

And the angel left.

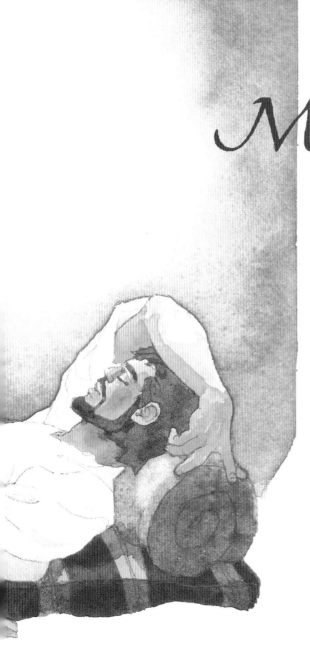

Mary was so happy about the news. She could hardly wait to tell Joseph.

But when Joseph heard about the angel's visit and the baby that Mary was going to have, he was not very excited.

Joseph worried about what people would think. He didn't want to hurt Mary, but he was not sure that they should be married. And that was what he had decided just before he went to sleep.

As Joseph slept, an angel appeared to him. "Do not be afraid to take Mary as your wife," the angel said. "Her child is from God. You will name him Jesus. He will save his people from their sins."

Joseph did as the angel told him.

The Emperor Augustus passed a new law. Every man had to go to his hometown to register. Joseph's family was from Bethlehem—the city of David. So, Mary and Joseph traveled to Bethlehem to be counted.

Clip, clop, clip, clop. The little donkey went up hill and down. The trip from Nazareth to Bethlehem was a very long way. Clip, clop, clip, clop. The donkey's steps grew slower and slower. Finally the three came to the town of Bethlehem.

People filled the streets of the little town. Many people had come to Bethlehem to register. In fact, there were so many people that all the guest rooms were full.

"Go away," said the innkeeper when Joseph knocked on the door. "We have no rooms!" He started to shut the door but he saw Mary. She looked so tired. He could tell that her baby was due at any time.

"Well, maybe I have a space where you can sleep. It is just a little stable out behind the inn. I have laid down fresh straw just today. You'll have to share it with the animals. But it is warm and dry."

The innkeeper led the way to the small stable. Joseph spread a blanket down across the sweet-smelling straw. Mary lay down to rest.

That night, with all the animals looking on, Mary gave birth to her firstborn son. She wrapped him in bands of cloth and laid him in a manger, because there had been no room for them at the inn.

On the night that Jesus was born, there were shepherds in the fields keeping watch over their sheep. The night was cold and they huddled close around the fire to keep warm.

Suddenly, instead of getting darker and darker, the sky began to get lighter and lighter. The shepherds were afraid.

An angel of the Lord appeared to the shepherds. "Do not be afraid. I bring you good news of a great joy that will be for all people. The Savior you have been waiting for was born this very night."

"How will we know him?" the shepherds asked.

"You will find the baby wrapped in bands of cloth, lying in a manger," said the angel.

And suddenly the night sky was filled with angels' voices. They sang, "Glory to God in the highest and peace to all people on earth!"

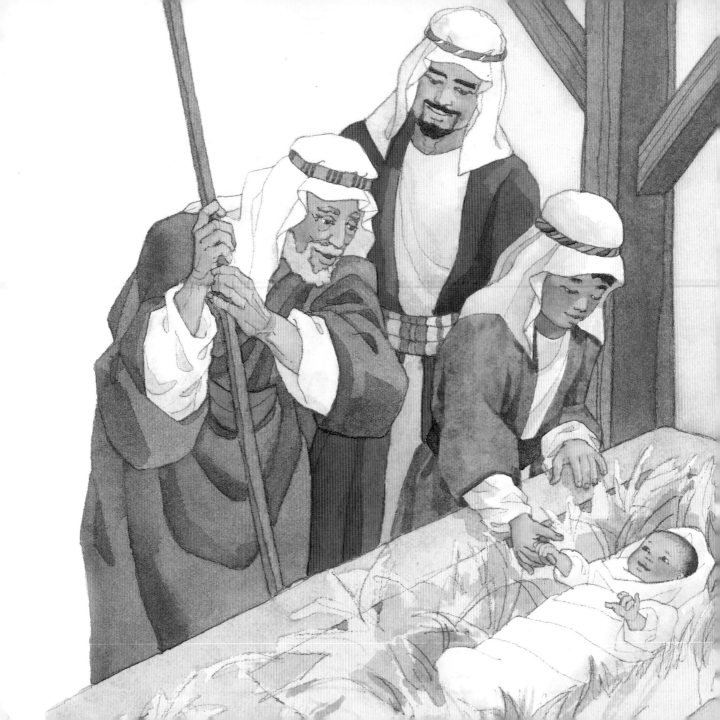

*W*hen the angels left, the shepherds turned to one another. "Let's go to Bethlehem and see this baby that the angels told us about."

So they set off for Bethlehem. There they found Mary, Joseph, and the baby Jesus just as the angels had told them.

The shepherds told Mary about the angels and all they had said.

When the shepherds left, they were so happy that they told everyone about the baby and the angel's song. All who heard were amazed.

The time came for Mary and Joseph to present their son at the Temple. As they walked up the great marble steps, they were greeted by a man named Simeon. Simeon was a very religious man. All his life he had been waiting to see the Savior that God would send.

Guided by the Holy Spirit, Simeon had come to the Temple this very day. When Simeon saw Mary and Joseph, he knew his prayers had been answered. Simeon went up to them. He reached for the baby Jesus and took him in his arms.

"This is the child that we have been waiting for. This is the one whom God has sent to bring glory to the nation," said Simeon. Then Simeon blessed the baby and the parents.

Mary and Joseph were amazed at what Simeon said to them.

While they were at the Temple, they also came across a woman whose name was Anna. She worshiped at the Temple. She worshiped night and day, never leaving. At the moment when Mary and Joseph brought their son to the Temple, she began to tell others about the child that God had sent to save God's people. Jesus was truly God's son.

*I*n a land far, far away from Bethlehem, there lived wise men who studied the stars. They watched the sky for signs that great events had happened.

One night, they saw something wonderful. A bright new star lit up the sky. "Come quick!" said one of the wise men. "You must see what I see!" He pointed high in the sky.

The men peered into the night. "It is a sign!" said the second. "A new king has been born!"

"We must go and find him," said the third. "But how will we know the way?"

"The star will lead us," said the first. So the three wise men set out on their journey. They did not know where they were going, but they knew they were going to see a king. So they brought fine gifts—gifts of gold, frankincense, and myrrh.

Every night the star went before them, leading the way. They traveled for a very long time. When they came to Jerusalem, the star was hovering almost overhead. The wise men knew they were very close. Surely the new king would be there.

The wise men searched the city for the new king. Everyone they saw they asked, "Where is the child who has been born king of the Jews? We have seen his star and have come to worship him."

But no one seemed to know where they could find him. They were almost ready to give up. But word spread and soon King Herod heard of the wise men's search.

"Hrrmph!" muttered the king. "What is this about a new king? I'm the only king! We'll soon see about this."

King Herod called together all of his most trusted advisors. They told him that the Scriptures said that indeed a king was to be born in Bethlehem. So the king sent word secretly to the wise men and called them to the palace for a meeting.

"Tell me about this new king that you search for," said the king, smiling very nicely. But he did not feel like smiling.

The wise men told King Herod about the bright new star and how it had led them to this place.

"Go and look for the child," said the king, "and when you find him, let me know so that I can come to worship him as well."

That night when the wise men left the palace, again the star went before them. It led them to a small house in the town of Bethlehem. There they found the child Jesus with his mother Mary.

The three wise men entered the house. They knelt down before the child and his mother. Then they opened their treasure chests, presenting gifts of gold, frankincense, and myrrh.

When the time came to return to their own land, however, the wise men did not send word back to King Herod. God had warned them in a dream that King Herod was not to be trusted. So they returned to their land by another road.